O Allah, send prayers upon our master Muhammad, the opener of what was closed, and the seal of what had preceded, the helper of the truth by the Truth, and the guide to Your straight path. May Allah send prayers upon his Family according to his grandeur and magnificent rank.

-SALĀT AL-FĀTĪH

Title: On Prayers Upon the Prophet
Author: Qāḍi 'Iyād b. Mūsa al-Yahsubi
Translator: Talut Dawood
Proofreading: Wordsmith
Interior Layout: Olivier Darbonville

ISBN: 978-1-952306-10-5

FIRST EDITION | FEBRUARY 2021

WWW.IMAMGHAZALI.ORG | INFO@IMAMGHAZALI.ORG

On Prayers ***Upon the Prophet***

Authored by

Qāḍi ʻIyād b. Mūsa al-Yahsubi

Translated by

Talut Dawood

Contents

Translator's Introduction / 7

Qāḍi 'Iyād / 11

SECTION 1
On the Meaning of Sending Prayers Upon Him 17

SECTION 2
On the Ruling of Sending Prayers Upon Him 19

SECTION 3
Situations in Which it is Recommended to Send Prayers and Peace Upon the Prophet ﷺ 24

SECTION 4
On the Method of Sending Prayers and Peace Upon Him........ 31

SECTION 5
On the Benefit of Sending Prayers and Peace Upon Him and of Supplicating for Him 39

SECTION 6
Censuring Those Who Do Not Send Prayers upon the Prophet ﷺ and the Sin That This Entails 44

SECTION 7
On His ﷺ Being Singled Out for Having the Prayer and Salutation Upon Him Delivered to Him 47

SECTION 8

Disagreement Over Sending Prayers Upon Other than the Prophet ﷺ and the Rest of the Prophets (peace be upon them) 50

SECTION 9

On the Ruling on Visiting Him, the Excellence of Those Who Visit Him and Greet Him With Peace, and the Method of That Greeting 56

SECTION 10

On the Etiquette of Entering the Noble Prophetic Masjid, Its Excellence and the Excellence of Madinah and Makkah 65

APPENDIX

Insights into Sending Prayers Upon the Prophet ﷺ / 77

Being with Allah and His Messenger ﷺ / 83

Translator's **Introduction**

All praise is due to Allah, the First; without a beginning, and the Last; without an end. Peace and prayers be upon the Prophet Muhammad (*ṣallallāhu ʿalaihi wa sallam*), the first Prophet on the Day of Judgement to offer intercession despite being the last Prophet sent, and upon his pure family, his blessed Companions, and all who follow their way upon the path of righteousness, until the day intercession begins with none other than the Prophet Muhammad (*ṣallallāhu ʿalaihi wa sallam*).

Al-Shifā bi Taʿrīf Ḥuqūq al-Muṣṭafā, directly translated as, 'The Remedy (or Cure) Through Recognizing the Rights of the Chosen One', is one of the most celebrated works in the genre of Shamā'il. It stands uniquely amongst the works of Qāḍī ʿIyād as his most celebrated effort–with many surviving manuscripts and commentaries found throughout the Islamic world. Shamā'il is a genre of works that deals with the life, characteristics, and descriptions of the Prophet (*ṣallallāhu ʿalaihi wa sallam*) and his station. There are many works in this genre, the most celebrated of which is *Al-Shamā'il al-Muḥammadiyyah,* which the Imam Ghazali Institute recently translated and published. Other works include commentaries and summaries of that nature, or hagiographical poems that recount the biography of the Prophet (*ṣallallāhu ʿalaihi wa sallam*) and render praise to the Prophetic station.

However, *Al-Shifā,* as it is called for short, stands alone as perhaps the most thorough work in this genre, dealing with both the descriptions of the Prophet (*ṣallallāhu ʿalaihi wa sallam*), his station and his perfections, and with the rulings pertaining to one's belief and treatment of him (*ṣallallāhu ʿalaihi wa sallam*). It is exhaustive in its treatment of the subject, expounding on topics that range from Allah's praise of the Prophet (*ṣallallāhu ʿalaihi wa sallam*) and his status and station before Him, to the obligation of loving him and what that entails. In short, the uniqueness of this work can be attributed to its holistic coverage of the Messenger (*ṣallallāhu ʿalaihi wa sallam*). Historically, this work took on a form of sacredness and was revered throughout the Muslim world. With that in mind, the Qāḍī's intention for this blessed work was more so to address, what he understood as, a real and practical need in his society. In today's context, it is our intention to continue the spirit of his desire outlined for us in his introduction:

> You have repeatedly asked me to write something which gathers together all that is necessary to acquaint the reader with the true stature of the Prophet, peace and blessings be upon him, with the esteem and respect

> which is due to him, and with the verdict regarding anyone who does not fulfill what his stature demands or who attempts to denigrate his supreme status—even by as much as a nail-paring. I have been asked to compile what our forebears and imams have said on this subject, and I will amplify it with ***ayāt*** from the Qur'an and other examples...Writing about this calls for the evaluation of the primary sources, examination of secondary sources, and investigation of the depths and details of the science of what is necessary for the Prophet, what should be attributed to him, and what is forbidden or permissible in respect of him; and deep knowledge of Messenger-ship and Prophethood and of the love, intimate friendship and the special qualities of the sublime rank.[1]

Although it has previously been translated into English in its entirety, our intention with this series is to attempt to bring out, for our readers, some of the most relevant smaller, yet critically important, topics related to the Prophet (*ṣallallāhu 'alaihi wa sallam*), his station, our duty towards him, and the benefit of loving him and fulfilling our duty towards him. Such a task has been made easier for us by the expert arrangement of the text in terms of its sections and subsections. Each larger section is divided into smaller subsections, which facilitates targeted publications that are small but great in benefit. It is our desire,

---

1 Iyad ibn Musa, Muhammad: Messenger of Allah: Ash-Shifā by Qadi 'Iyad , translated by Aisha Abdarrahman Bewley, vi.

with having isolated smaller and somewhat easier 'quick-reads', as they are called, that readers may be inspired to complete a full reading of the noble Qāḍī's entire work.

Talut Dawood
Mexico City, Mexico
February 2021

Qāḍi 'Iyād

The Imām, the unique Ḥāfiẓ, Shaykh al-Islām, 'Allāmah, Qāḍi Abū al-Faḍl 'Iyād b. Mūsa b. 'Iyād b. 'Umar b. Mūsa b. 'Iyād al-Yahsubi al-Andalūsi al-Sibti al-Māliki was born in the year 476/1083–84, six months after the Almoravid takeover of the city. His ancestors left Andalus for Fez and then settled in Ceuta. At the age of 22, Qāḍi 'Iyād obtained a license (*ijāzah*) from Ḥāfiẓ Abū 'Alī al-Ghasāni. This allowed Qāḍi 'Iyād to take knowledge from him. The Qāḍi had otherwise not studied the Islāmic sciences at an early age.

He left Ceuta on two occasions, one of which was to travel to Andalus seeking out scholars with whom he could take knowledge. Between 507/1113 and 508/1114 the Qāḍi visited Cordoba, Almeria, Murcia, and Granada. During this time, he learned Ḥadith from the famed scholar, Qāḍi Abū 'Alī b. Sukrah al-Sadafi. Qāḍi 'Iyād stayed with him closely. He also took Ḥadīth from Abū Baḥr b. al-'Ās, Muḥammad b. Ḥamdayn, Abū al-Ḥusayn Sirāj al-Saghīr, Abū Muḥammad b. 'Attab, Hishām b. Aḥmad and many other scholars. He learned jurisprudence (*fiqh*) from Abū

'Abdullah Muḥammad b. 'Isa al-Tamīmī and Qāḍi Muḥammad b. 'Abdullāh al-Masili.

The Qāḍi was first appointed judge of Ceuta in 515/1121 and served in his position until 531/1136. He would later serve again in Cueta from 539–543/1145–48. His tenure as a judge in Cueta was probably his most productive period; his casework created the foundations for his works in jurisprudence (*fiqh*). Khalaf b. Shakwal said of him:

> He is among the people of knowledge and polymaths, of great intelligence and understanding. He performed the duties of a judge in Ceuta for a long time, in which he earned a praiseworthy reputation. Then he travelled from there for a judgeship in Granada. However, he did not stay there long. Thereafter, he came to us in Cordoba and we took from him.

The jurist (*faqīh*) Muḥammad b. Ḥammadah al-Sibti said:

> The Qāḍi began training at the age of twenty-eight years and assumed judgeship at the age of thirty-five. He was lenient, but not weak, [and] fierce in defence of the truth. He learned jurisprudence (fiqh) from Abū 'Abdullah al-Tamīmī and accompanied Abū Isḥāq b. Ja'far. No one in Ceuta wrote more works than him during his time. He wrote the book 'Al-Shifā' fi Sharāf al-Mustafa', 'Tartīb al-Madārik wa Taqrīb al-Masālik fī Dhikr Fuqahā' Madhab Mālik', a multi-volume work, 'Kitāb al-'Aqīdah', 'Kitāb Sharḥ Ḥadīth Umm Zar'', the book 'Jāmi' al-Tārīkh' and others.

Many scholars narrate from Qāḍi 'Iyād. Among them are Imām 'Abdullah b. Muḥammad al-'Ashīri, Abū Ja'far b. al-Qasir al-Gharnāti, al-Ḥāfiẓ Khalaf b. Bashakwal, Abū Muḥammad b. 'Ubayd Allah al-Hijri, Muḥammad b. al-Ḥasan al-Jābirī and his son, Qāḍi Muḥammad b. 'Iyād, the Qāḍi of Denia (in Spain).

Qāḍi b. Khalkhan said, 'The teachers of Qāḍi 'Iyād number around one hundred. He passed away during Ramaḍan 544/December-January 1149–50.' Conversely, it has also been reported that he died in Jumada al-Ākhirah of the same year, in Marrakesh. His son passed away in the year 575 AH.

Ibn Bashakwal said, 'Qāḍi 'Iyād passed away to the west of his hometown, in the middle of the year 544 AH." His son, Qāḍi Muḥammad, said, 'He passed away in the middle of the night, on Friday 9 Jumada al-Ākhirah. He was buried in Marrakesh in the year 544 AH.'

I [al-Dhahabi] say, 'it has reached me that he was killed by an arrow for his denial that Ibn Tumart was infallible'.

Some of the Qāḍi's well-known works are:

1. Al-Shifā' bi Ta'rīf Ḥuqūq al-Mustafā – the Shifa' remains one of the most commentated books of Islām.

2. Tartīb al-Madārik wa Taqrīb al-Masālik li Ma'rifat A'lām Madhab Mālik.

3. Ikmāl al-Mu`lim bi Fawa'id Muslim – Qāḍi `Iyād's own commentary was expounded upon heavily by Imām al-Nawawi in his commentary of Saḥiḥ Muslim.

4. Al-I`lām bi Ḥudūd Qawā'id al-Islām – a work on the five pillars of Islām.
5. Al-Ilma` ilā Ma`rifa Usūl al-Riwāyah wa Taqyīd al-Sama` – a detailed work on the science of Ḥadīth.
6. Mashāriq al-Anwār `ala Saḥiḥ al-Athar – a work based on the Muwaṭā of Imām Mālik, Saḥiḥ Al-Bukhāri of Imām Bukhāri, and Saḥiḥ Muslim by Imām Muslim.
7. Al-Tanbihāt al-Mustanbaṭah `ala al-Kutub al-Mudawwanah wa al-Mukhtalaṭah.
8. Daqā`iq al-Akhbar fi Dhikr al-Jannah wa al-Nār – a work describing the joys of Heaven (*Jannah*) and the horrors of Hell (*Jahannam*).

ON PRAYERS UPON THE PROPHET

On the Rulings of
Sending Prayers
Upon the Prophet ﷺ,
What is Obligatory from Them
and Their Benefits

SECTION ONE

On the Meaning of Sending Prayers Upon Him

Allah (Exalted is He) has said, "Indeed, Allah and His Angels send prayers upon the Prophet. O you who believe! Send prayers upon him and extend him a worthy salutation" (*al-Aḥzāb*, 33:56).

Ibn 'Abbas said, "The meaning (of this verse) is that Allah and His Angels bless the Prophet ﷺ." It has also been said that it means, "Indeed, Allah has mercy upon His Prophet ﷺ, and the Angels supplicate for him." Al-Mubrid said, "The root meaning of *ṣalāh* (prayers) is to show mercy. Thus, (prayers) from Allah are mercy and prayers from the Angels are compassion and seeking for Allah to have mercy (on the person)."

The prayers of the Angels upon the one who is sitting and waiting for the prayer have been narrated in several hadiths. The Angels will say, "O Allah! Forgive him. O Allah! Have mercy on him." In this sense, it is a supplication.

Abu Bakr al-Qushayri said, "The prayer of Allah (Exalted is He) upon other than the Prophet ﷺ is mercy, while His prayer upon the Prophet ﷺ is an ennoblement and an increase in honour."

Abu al-'Aliyah said, "The prayer of Allah is His praising him in the presence of the Angels, and the prayer of the Angels is supplication."

Qāḍī Abu al-Fadl[2] says, "In the hadith where the Prophet ﷺ taught the manner of sending prayers upon him, he distinguished between the word *ṣalāh* and the word *barakah*. This indicates that they have two distinct meanings."

As for the salutation that Allah (Exalted is He) ordered His servants to extend him, Qāḍī Abu Bakr ibn Bakir said, "This verse was revealed to the Prophet ﷺ, and Allah ordered his Companions to send salutations upon him. Likewise, those who came after him were ordered to send salutations upon the Prophet ﷺ at his grave and whenever he is mentioned."

There are three points of view regarding the meaning of 'peace'. The first is that it means, "May peace be with you and in your favour." In this sense, *salām* is a verbal noun. The second is that it means, "May *al-Salām* take charge of and assume responsibility of your protection, and guardianship.' In this sense, *al-Salām* would be the Name of Allah. The third is that the meaning is surrender and obeisance, as indicated in Allah's words when he says, "Nay! By your Lord! They will not believe until they make you a judge over that which occurs between them, and then do not find within themselves any rejection to what you have decided and they surrender completely" (*al-Nisā'*, 4:65).

---

2 Qāḍī 'Iyāḍ.

SECTION TWO

On the Ruling of Sending Prayers Upon Him

Sending prayers upon the Prophet ﷺ is a universal obligation that is not restricted to a certain time or place. This obligation is established by Allah's command to send prayers upon the Prophet ﷺ, and the unanimous interpretation of the imams and scholars that indicate an obligation.

However, Abu Ja'far al-Tabari said that the indication of the verse, according to him, is that it is recommended. He claimed that there is consensus on this. But perhaps he was referring to reciting the prayers more than once.

The obligatory amount of prayer upon the Prophet ﷺ that exonerates the person of the error and sin of abandoning an obligation is one time, just like bearing witness to the Prophethood of the Prophet ﷺ. Beyond that, reciting it more than once is recommended and encouraged both in the Sunnah of Islam and as an emblem of its people.

Qāḍī Abu al-Hasan ibn al-Qusar said, "The dominant opinion among our companions is that it is a universal obligation, and that it is obligatory for a person to recite it once in his life if he is able." Qāḍī Abu Bakr ibn Bakir said, "Allah obligated His creation to send prayers upon His Prophet ﷺ, and to extend him a worthy salutation. He did not restrict this to a specific time, so it is necessary that an individual recite it a lot and that he does not neglect it."

Qāḍī Abu Muhammad ibn Nasr said, "Sending prayers upon the Prophet ﷺ is a universal obligation." Qāḍī Abu Abdullah Muhammad ibn Sa'id said, "Mālik, his companions, and other scholars opined that sending prayers upon the Prophet ﷺ is a universal obligation with the objective of faith. It is not restricted to the prayer alone. Furthermore, if someone sends one prayer upon him in his life, that obligation has been fulfilled by him."

The companions of al-Shāfiʿī, on the other hand, said, "The obligatory prayer upon the Prophet ﷺ is that which Allah (Exalted is He) and His Messenger ﷺ commanded. That is in the prayer." They also said, "As for outside of the prayer, there is no difference of opinion over the fact that it is not obligatory."

As for in the prayer, the two Imams Abu Ja'far al-Tabari and al-Tahawi, along with others, have reported a consensus among early and late scholars of the Ummah that sending prayers upon the Prophet ﷺ in the *tashahhud* is not obligatory. Al-Shāfiʿī went alone in his opinion, saying, "If someone does not send prayers upon the Prophet ﷺ after the *tashahhud* in the last *rak'ah*, before giving *salām*, his prayer is invalidated. If he sends prayers upon him before that, it does not suffice him."

Al-Shāfiʿī has no predecessor in this opinion, nor was he following any Sunnah. He therefore received much criticism regarding his stance on this issue, because he opposed the entire body of scholars who had preceded him. He was reviled for his disagreement with the previous scholars by more than one scholar, including al-Tabari and al-Qushayri.

Abu Bakr ibn al-Mundhir said, "It is preferable that one does not perform any prayer except that he sends prayers in it upon the Messenger of Allah ﷺ. If someone abandons it, his prayer is valid according to the *madhhab* of Mālik, the People of Madinah, Sufyan al-Thawri, the People of Kufa among the *Ahl al-Ra'y* and others. This is the opinion of the majority of the people of knowledge."

It has been narrated that Mālik and Sufyan said, "It is preferable to recite it (the prayer) in the final *tashahhud*, and that the one who abandons it in the *tashahhud* is sinful. Al-Shāfi'ī, on the other hand, opposed the rest, obligating that one who leaves it in prayer to repeat the prayer." Ishaq ibn Rahwayh said that repeating the prayer is obligatory upon the person who leaves out the prayer upon the Prophet ﷺ intentionally, but not upon the one who leaves it out of forgetfulness.

Abu Muhammad ibn Abi Zayd narrated from Muhammad ibn al-Mawwaz that sending prayers upon the Prophet ﷺ is an obligation. Abu Muhammad said, "He meant that it is not from the obligatory acts of the prayer." Muhammad ibn 'Abd al-Hakam and others said – and Ibn al-Qussar and 'Abd al-Wahhab narrated – that Muhammad ibn al-Mawwaz saw it as an obligatory act of the prayer, as did Al-Shāfi'ī. Abu Ya'la al-'Abdi al-Māliki narrated that there are three opinions in the *madhhab* regarding sending prayers to the Prophet ﷺ during the prayer: that it is obligatory, that it is Sunnah and that it is recommended.

Al-Khattabi differed with the companions of al-Shāfi'ī and other Shāfi'īs regarding this issue. He said, "It is not an obligatory act of the prayer. This is the opinion of the majority of the jurists apart from al-Shāfi'ī. I do not know of anyone that he could be following in that."

The evidence that it is not among the obligatory acts of the prayer is the practice of those who preceded al-Shāfi'ī, whose consensus is that it is not obligatory. The scholars had criticized al-Shāfi'ī greatly for this issue. In fact, the *tashahhud* that al-Shāfi'ī preferred was the one reported by Ibn Mas'ud, which the Prophet ﷺ taught him and does not contain any prayer upon the Prophet ﷺ. Likewise, none of those who narrated the *tashahhud* from the Prophet ﷺ, such as Abu Hurairah, Ibn 'Abbas, Jabir, Ibn 'Umar, Abu Sa'id al-Khudrī, Abu Musa al-Ashʿarī and Abdullah ibn al-Zubayr, mentioned any prayer upon the Prophet ﷺ as part of it.

Ibn 'Abbas and Jabir said, "The Prophet ﷺ would teach us the *tashahhud* like he would teach us chapters of the Qur'an." Abu Sa'id al-Khudrī narrated the same. Ibn 'Umar said, "Abu Bakr used to teach us the *tashahhud* upon the *minbar*, just as children are taught in their classrooms." 'Umar ibn al-Khattab (may Allah be pleased with him) would also teach it upon the *minbar*.

There is also the hadith, "There is no prayer for he who does not send prayers upon me."[3] Ibn al-Qussar said,

---

3 Sunan Ibn Mājah.

"It means that one's prayer is not complete without it, or it means that there is no prayer for the one who has not sent prayers upon the Prophet ﷺ at least once in his life." However, all the scholars of Hadith have declared this hadith as weak.

There is another hadith narrated by Abu Ja'far, on the authority of Ibn Mas'ud, that the Prophet ﷺ said, "If someone prays a prayer in which he has not sent prayers upon me and the people of my house, his prayer will not be accepted." Regarding this hadith, al-Daraqutni said, "The correct position is that they are the words of Abu Ja'far Muhammad ibn 'Ali ibn al-Husayn, who said, 'If I pray a prayer in which I do not send prayers upon the Prophet ﷺ and upon the people of his house, I would not consider my prayer as complete.'"

SECTION THREE

Situations in Which it is Recommended to Send Prayers and Peace Upon the Prophet ﷺ

Regarding the situations in which it is recommended to send prayers and peace upon the Prophet ﷺ, and in which it is encouraged, one of them is the *tashahhud* in the prayer, as we have mentioned. The proper time is after the *tashahhud* and before the supplication. Fadalah ibn 'Ubayd said, "The Prophet ﷺ heard a man supplicating in his prayer who had not sent prayers upon the Prophet ﷺ. The Prophet ﷺ said, 'He has been hasty.' Then he called him over and said to him and others, 'When one of you prays, let him begin by praising and extolling Allah. Then, let him send prayers upon the Prophet ﷺ. Then, let him supplicate after that for whatever he wants.'[4] It has also been narrated with a different chain of transmission that he said, "By glorifying Allah."[5] And that is the most authentic narration.

---

4 Sunan al-Tirmidhī

5 Sunan Ibn Mājah

'Umar ibn al-Khattab (may Allah be pleased with him) said, "Supplication and prayers are suspended between Heaven and Earth. No part of them ascend to Allahntil prayers are sent upon the Prophet ﷺ."[6] In another narration, 'Ali narrated from the Prophet ﷺ something with the same meaning. And in another narration, the Prophet ﷺ added, "and upon the family of Muhammad."

It was also narrated that supplications are veiled until the supplicant sends prayers upon the Prophet ﷺ. Ibn Mas'ud said, "Whenever one of you wants to ask Allah for something, let him begin by praising and extolling Him as He deserves, then let him send prayers upon the Prophet ﷺ, then let him ask, for this (way) is more worthy and better suited for a reward."

Jabir (may Allah be pleased with him) narrates that the Messenger of Allah ﷺ said, "Do not treat me like the water skin of the rider. The rider fills his water skin and then puts it down. Then, he picks up his possessions. Then, if he needs to drink, he drinks and if he needs to perform ablution, he performs it. If not, he leaves it. Rather, mention me at the beginning of your supplication, in the middle of it, and at the end.'[7]

Ibn 'Ata' said, "Supplications have pillars, wings, means, and times. If one completes its pillars, it becomes strong. If he conforms to its wings, it flies into the sky. If his supplication corresponds to its times, it succeeds.

---

6 Sunan al-Tirmidhī

7 Bazzār, Abū Yaʿlā and al-Bayhaqī

And if he takes its means, it is favoured. Its pillars are the presence of heart, etiquette, submission, humility, and the heart's attachment to Allah and detachment from intermediary means. Its wings are sincerity. Its time is the early (pre-dawn) morning. Its means are prayers upon the Prophet ﷺ."

In another hadith, the Prophet ﷺ is reported to have said, "A supplication made between two prayers (upon the Prophet) is not rejected." In another hadith, he says, "Every supplication is veiled from Heaven. Then, when the supplicant sends prayers upon the Prophet ﷺ, it ascends."

The supplication of Ibn 'Abbas, which was narrated by Hansh, ends with, "Accept my supplication. Then begin with prayers upon the Prophet ﷺ, saying, 'O Allah! I ask You that You send blessings upon Muhammad – your slave, prophet, and messenger – with a prayer that is superior to any prayer that You have sent upon anyone in all creation. *Āmīn*.'"

Other situations for sending prayers upon him is when he is mentioned, when hearing his name, when writing it, and at the time of the *adhān*. The Prophet ﷺ said, "May he regret in whose presence I am mentioned and he does not send prayers upon me."[8]

However, Ibn Habīb disliked that the Prophet ﷺ should be mentioned at the time of slaughter. Sahnun disliked sending prayers upon him as an expression of amazement. He said, "One should not send prayers upon

---

8 Saḥīḥ Muslim

him, except when one anticipates and seeks a reward." Asbagh narrated that Ibn al-Qasim said, "There are two situations in which only Allah is mentioned: at the time of slaughter and when one sneezes. In those two times, one should not say, after mentioning Allah, 'Muhammad is the Messenger of Allah.' However, if, after mentioning Allah, one was to say, 'May Allah bless Muhammad,' it would not amount to mentioning him alongside Allah."

Ashhab said, "It is not proper to limit the prayers upon the Prophet ﷺ to a specific time."

Al-Nasā'ī narrated from Aws ibn Aws that the Prophet ﷺ commanded that people send copious prayers upon him on the Day of Jumu'ah.

Another situation for sending prayers and peace upon him is when entering the *Masjid*. Abu Ishaq ibn Sha'ban said, "It is necessary for the one who enters the *Masjid* to send prayers and blessings upon the Prophet ﷺ and upon his family, to invoke mercy upon them, and to extend them a worthy salutation. He should then say, 'O Allah! Forgive me my sins, and open for me the doors of Your mercy.' And when he leaves, he should do the same, except that, when leaving, instead of 'Your mercy,' he should say, 'Your grace.'"

Regarding Allah's words, "When you enter houses, send peace upon yourselves" (*al-Nūr*, 24:61), 'Amr ibn Dinar said, "If there is no one in the house, then say, 'Peace be upon the Prophet ﷺ and the mercy and blessings of Allah. Peace be upon us and upon the pious servants of Allah. Peace be upon the People of the House and the mercy and blessings of Allah.'" Ibn 'Abbas said, "The meaning of 'houses' here is mosques."

Al-Nakha'i said, "If there is no one in the *Masjid*, say, 'Peace be upon the Messenger of Allah ﷺ.' And if there is no one in the house, say, 'Peace be upon us and the pious servants of Allah.'"

'Alqamah said, "When I enter a *Masjid*, I say, 'Peace be upon you, O Prophet, and the mercy and blessings of Allah. May Allah and His Angels send prayers upon Muhammad ﷺ.'" Ka'b said something similar, saying, "When you enter or exit..." The rest is the same, except he did not mention the final prayer upon the Prophet ﷺ. As evidence for this practice, Ibn Sha'ban mentioned the hadith of Fatimah bint Rasulillah ﷺ that the Prophet ﷺ would do so when entering the *Masjid*.[9]

Abu Bakr ibn 'Amr ibn Hazm mentioned a similar matter, and he also mentioned peace and mercy. This last hadith was mentioned by al-Qasim. He mentioned a variety of different wordings for it.

Another situation for sending prayers upon the Prophet ﷺ is upon the defunct person being prayed over. Abu Umamah mentioned that it is from the Sunnah.

One of the other situations for sending prayers upon him, which the *Ummah* has been steadfast at performing, and which no one has criticized, is to send prayers upon the Prophet ﷺ and upon his family in letters, after writing the *basmalah*. This practice did not exist in the first generations. It was started during the rule of Bani Hashim. People in all regions of the earth adopted it and were steadfast in it. Some of them even close out their written works with it.

---

9 Sunan al-Tirmidhī

The Prophet ﷺ said, "If someone sends prayers upon me in a book, the Angels will continue to seek forgiveness for him as long as my name is in that book."[10]

Another situation for sending peace upon the Prophet ﷺ is in the *tashahhud* during the prayer. Abdullah ibn Mas'ud narrates that the Prophet ﷺ said, "When one of you prays, let him say, 'Salutations, prayers and good things are all for Allah. Peace be upon you, O Prophet, and the mercy and blessings of Allah. Peace be upon us and upon the pious servants of Allah.' If you say this, your salutation will reach every pious slave in the Heavens and the Earth." Thus, this is one of the places for sending peace upon him. The Sunnah is to do so in the first part of the *tashahhud.*

Mālik has also narrated that Ibn 'Umar would say this after he had completed his *tashahhud* and before he would give *salām* to end the prayer. Mālik is reported in *Al-Mabsūt* to have preferred that it be recited before giving *salām* to end the prayer.

Muhammad ibn Maslamah said, "He meant that which has been narrated about 'A'ishah and Ibn 'Umar that they both would say (before giving *salām* to end the prayer), "Peace be upon you, O Prophet, and the mercy and blessings of Allah. Peace be upon us and upon the pious servants of Allah. Peace be upon you."

The people of knowledge considered it preferable that a person make an intention when he gives *salām*, thereby

---

10 Al-Ṭabarānī in *al-Awsaṭ*

greeting every pious slave in the Heaven and the Earth, among the Angels, the Children of Adam, and the jinn.

In his *Majmū'*, Mālik said, "I like that when the Imam gives *salām,* that the follower should say, 'Peace be upon the Prophet and the mercy and blessings of Allah. Peace be upon us and upon the pious servants of Allah. Peace be upon you.'"

SECTION FOUR

On the Method of Sending Prayers and Peace Upon Him

Abu Hamid al-Sa'idi narrated that the Companions said, "O Messenger of Allah! How should we send prayers upon you?" He replied, "Say: O Allah! Send prayers upon Muhammad, his wives, and his offspring, just as You have sent prayers upon Ibrahim. And bless Muhammad, his wives, and his offspring, just as You have blessed the family of Ibrahim. Indeed, You are worthy of all praise and very Majestic.'"[11]

With another chain of transmission, Mālik narrates that Abu Mas'ud al-Ansari said that the Prophet ﷺ said, "Say: 'O Allah! Send prayers upon Muhammad and the family of Muhammad, just as You sent prayers upon the family of Ibrahim. And bless Muhammad and the family of Muhammad, just as You blessed the family of Ibrahim from amongst all the worlds. Indeed, You are worthy of all praise and very Majestic. And you already know how to send salutations.'"

In another narration from Ka'b ibn 'Ujrah, the Prophet ﷺ said, "O Allah! Send prayers upon Muhammad and

11 Mālik in *al-Muwaṭṭa'*

the family of Muhammad, just as You sent prayers upon Ibrahim... And bless Muhammad and the family of Muhammad, just as You blessed Ibrahim..."[12]

'Uqbah ibn 'Amr narrates, "O Allah! Send prayers upon Muhammad the Unlettered Prophet, and the family of Muhammad."[13]

Abu Sa'id al-Khudri narrates, "O Allah! Send prayers upon Muhammad, your slave and Messenger, the Unlettered Prophet..."[14]

'Ali said, "I learned the following words directly from the Messenger of Allah ﷺ, who said, 'I took them directly from Jibrīl, who said, "They descended from the Mighty Lord like this:

> O Allah! Send prayers upon Muhammad and the family of Muhammad, just as you sent prayers upon Ibrahim and the family of Ibrahim. Indeed, You are worthy of all praise, very Majestic. O Allah! Bless Muhammad and the family of Muhammad, just as You blessed Ibrahim and the family of Ibrahim. Indeed, You are worthy of all praise, very Majestic. O Allah! Show mercy to Muhammad and the family of Muhammad, just as You showed mercy to Ibrahim and the family of Ibrahim. Indeed, You are worthy of all praise, very Majestic. O Allah! Love Muhammad and the family of Muhammad, just as You loved Ibrahim and the family of Ibrahim. Indeed, You are

---

12 Narrated by the authors of the six books of Hadith.

13 Ibn Ḥibbān, Dāraquṭnī and al-Bayhaqī

14 Al-Ḥākim

> worthy of all praise, very Majestic. Send peace upon Muhammad and the family of Muhammad, just as You sent peace upon Ibrahim and the family of Ibrahim. Indeed, You are worthy off all praise, very Majestic."

Abu Hurairah narrated that the Prophet ﷺ said, "If someone wishes to obtain the greatest reward when he sends prayers upon us (the people of the house), he should say, 'O Allah! Bless Muhammad the Prophet, his wives the Mothers of the Believers, his offspring, and the people of his house, just as you sent prayers upon Ibrahim. Indeed, You are worthy of all praise, very Majestic.'"[15]

In another hadith, Zayd ibn Kharijah al-Ansari asked the Prophet ﷺ, "How should we send prayers upon you?" The Prophet ﷺ replied, "Pray, exert yourself in supplication, then say, 'O, Allah! Bless Muhammad and the family of Muhammad, just as You blessed Ibrahim. Indeed, You are worthy of all praise, very Majestic.'"[16]

Salamah al-Kindi said, "'Ali would teach us the following prayer upon the Prophet ﷺ:

> O Allah! Leveller of the Earth and Creator of the Heavens, send the noblest of Your prayers, the most excellent of Your blessings, and the most gracious of Your blessings upon Muhammad, Your slave and Messenger, the opener of that which was closed, the Seal of what went before, the one who proclaims the Truth by the Truth,

---

15 Sunan Abū Dāwūd and al-Ṭabarānī

16 Al-Daylamī

the one who repels the armies of falsehood, as was his responsibility. He took it upon himself, through Your command, to obey You, earning Your satisfaction, bearing Your revelation, upholding Your covenant, and faithfully delivering Your command until he had lit a lamp for the seekers of the favours of Allah that would cause them to obtain their objective. By him, hearts were guided after being submerged in the seditions of sin. He clarified the evident signs, the luminous decrees, and the lights of Islam. He is Your trustworthy confidant, the treasurer of Your priceless knowledge, Your witness on the Day of Judgement, and the one who You have sent as a blessing; who You sent as a mercy and the Messenger of Truth. O Allah! Admit Him into Your Eden, reward Him with multitudes of good out of Your grace – endowments free of all difficulty – by causing him to obtain Your reward therein and multitudes of Your amazing gifts. O Allah! Elevate his works above the works of other people, make his status and position with You honourable, perfect for him his light. Grant him, from those to whom You have sent him, people of accepted testimonies (of faith), pleasing words, just judgement, guided steps, and immense proofs."

Another prayer upon the Prophet ﷺ that has been reported from 'Ali is as follows:

"Allah and His Angels sent prayers upon the Prophet. O you who believe! Send prayers upon him and extend him a worthy salutation" (al-Aḥzāb, 33:56). I comply with Your command, O Allah, my Lord, and seek to please

> You. May the prayers of Allah the Beneficent and Merciful, of the Angels drawn near, of the prophets and Siddīqīn, of the martyrs and the pious, and of all that has glorified You, O Lord of the worlds, be upon Muhammad ibn Abdullah, the Seal of the Prophets, the Master of the Messengers, the Imam of the God-conscious, the Messenger of the Lord of the worlds, the witness and bearer of glad tidings, the caller to You by Your permission, and the illuminated lamp. And may peace be upon him.

The following prayer upon the Prophet ﷺ has been narrated from Abdullah ibn Mas'ud:

> O Allah! Single out for Your prayers, blessings and mercy, the Master of the Messengers, the Imam of the God-conscious, and the Seal of the Prophets, Muhammad, Your slave and Messenger, the Imam of all good, and the Messenger of mercy. O Allah! Place him in the praiseworthy station, for which the first and the last will envy him. O Allah! Send prayers upon Muhammad and upon the family of Muhammad, just as You have sent prayers upon Ibrahim. Indeed, You are worthy of all praise, very Majestic. And bless Muhammad and the family Muhammad, just as You have blessed Ibrahim. Indeed, You are worthy of all praise, very Majestic.

Al-Hasan al-Basrī would say, "If someone wants to drink the fullest glass from the pond of the Chosen One ﷺ, let him say, 'O Allah! Send prayers upon Muhammad, his family, his Companions, his children, his wives, his descendants, the people of his house, his in-laws, his helpers, his adherents, his lovers, his *Ummah*, and upon us all along with them, O Most Merciful of the merciful."

Tawus narrated that Ibn 'Abbas would say, "O Allah! Accept the Greatest Intercession of Muhammad ﷺ, raise him to the highest rank, and grant him his requests in the Hereafter and in this world, just as You granted the requests of Ibrahim and Musa."

Wuhayb ibn al-Warad would say during his supplication, "O Allah! Grant Muhammad ﷺ the best of that which he has requested for himself. Grant Muhammad ﷺ the best of that which anyone in Your creation has requested for him. And grant Muhammad ﷺ the best of that for which You will be requested until the Day of Judgement."

It has also been narrated that Ibn Mas'ud (may Allah be pleased with him) said, "When you send prayers upon the Prophet ﷺ, make it the most excellent prayer upon him (that you are able to do). You do not know if perhaps it will be presented to him. Say:

> O Allah! Single out for Your prayer, mercy, and blessings the Master of the Messengers, the Imam of the God-conscious and the Seal of the Prophets, Muhammad, Your slave and Messenger; the Imam of all good, the leader of all good, and the Messenger of mercy. O Allah! Cause him to reach the praiseworthy station in which he will be envied by the first of the last. Send prayers upon Muhammad and the family of Muhammad, just as you sent prayers upon Ibrahim. Indeed, You are worthy of all praise, very Majestic. O Allah! Bless Muhammad and the family of Muhammad, just as you blessed Ibrahim. Indeed, You are worthy of all praise, very Majestic."

There are many other narrations that implicate extending the prayer and praising the people of the house and others.

The words of Ibn Mas'ud when he says, "And you already know how to send salutations" refers to the salutation that was taught in the *tashahhud*, "Peace be upon you, O Prophet, and the mercy and blessings of Allah. Peace be upon us and upon the pious servants of Allah."

The *tashahhud* reported from 'Ali contains the following salutation:

> Peace be upon the Prophet of Allah. Peace be upon the prophets of Allah and His Messengers. Peace be upon the Messenger of Allah. Peace be upon Muhammad ibn Abdullah. Peace be upon us and upon the believing men and women, those who are absent, and those who are present. O Allah! Forgive the people of the house, forgive me and my parents, and their children, and have mercy on them both. Peace be upon us and upon the pious servants of Allah. Peace be upon you, O Prophet, and the mercy and blessings of Allah.

In this hadith from 'Ali, there has come a supplication for forgiveness for the Prophet ﷺ. In the hadith on sending prayers upon him that preceded, there is a supplication for him to receive mercy. This has only been mentioned in this hadith, and not in any recognized hadiths attributable to the Prophet ﷺ. However, Abu 'Umar ibn 'Abd al-Barr and others have opined that one should not supplicate for the Prophet ﷺ to receive mercy. Rather, one should only supplicate for him through sending prayers and asking for the blessings for which he has been singled out. For others, one should supplicate for mercy and forgiveness.

Nevertheless, Abu Muhammad ibn Abi Zayd mentioned in the prayer upon the Prophet ﷺ the following words: "O Allah! Send mercy upon Muhammad and the family of Muhammad, just as You sent mercy upon Ibrahim and the family of Ibrahim." Yet this was not mentioned in any authentic hadith. His evidence was the words in the salutation (of the *tashahhud*), "Peace be upon you, O Prophet and the mercy and blessings of Allah."

SECTION FIVE

On the Benefit of Sending Prayers and Peace Upon Him and of Supplicating for Him

It has been narrated that Abdullah ibn 'Umar said, "I heard the Messenger of Allah ﷺ say, 'When you hear the *adhān*, repeat what the *mu'adhdhin* says. Then send prayers upon me, for if anyone send prayers upon me once, Allah sends ten prayers upon him. Then request for me *al-wasīlah*. It is a station in Paradise that has been reserved for only one slave from among the servants of Allah, and I hope that I will be him. My intercession is necessary for anyone that requests *al-wasīlah* for me."[17]

Anas ibn Mālik narrated that the Prophet ﷺ said, "If someone sends one prayer upon me, Allah sends ten prayers upon him, He erases for him ten mistakes, and He raises him ten degrees."[18] In another narration, he added, "And He records for him ten good deeds."

Anas narrated that the Prophet ﷺ said, "Jibrīl summoned me and said, 'If someone sends one prayer upon

---

17 Saḥīḥ Muslim, Sunan al-Nasā'ī, Sunan Abū Dāwūd, and Sunan al-Tirmidhī

18 Al-Bayhaqī

you, Allah will send ten prayers upon him, and He will raise him ten degrees.'"[19]

The same hadith was narrated by 'Abd al-Rahman ibn 'Awf, who said that the Prophet ﷺ said, "I met Jibrīl and he said to me, 'I am giving you the glad tidings that Allah (Exalted is He) has said, "If someone greets you, I greet them. And if someone sends prayers upon you, I send prayers upon him."'"[20] Similar hadiths have been narrated from Abu Hurairah and Mālik ibn Aws ibn al-Hadathan.

'Ubayd Allah ibn Abi Talhah narrates from Zayd ibn al-Khabbab that the latter said, "I heard the Prophet ﷺ say, 'If someone says, "O Allah! Send prayers upon Muhammad and place him in the station of nearness to You on the Day of Judgement," my intercession will be obligatory for him.'"[21]

Ibn Mas'ud narrated that the Prophet ﷺ said, "The closest person to me on the Day of Judgement will be the one who has sent the most prayers upon me."[22]

Abu Hurairah narrated that the Prophet ﷺ said, "If someone sends prayers upon me in a book, the Angels will continue to seek forgiveness for him as long as my name is in that book."[23]

---

19 Ibn Abī Shaybah

20 Al-Ḥākim

21 Al-Bukhārī, *al-Adab al-Mufrad*

22 Sunan al-Tirmidhī; Saḥīḥ Ibn Ḥibbān

23 Al-Ṭabarānī in *al-Awsaṭ*

'Amir ibn Rabi'ah said, "I heard the Prophet ﷺ say, 'If someone sends one prayer upon me, the Angels will send equal blessings upon him. So let the slave either perform a little or a lot.'"[24]

Ubayy ibn Ka'b narrated that the Messenger of Allah ﷺ stood up after a quarter of the night had passed and said, "O people! Remember Allah! The earthquake has come. It will be followed by the Hour." So, Ubayy ibn Ka'b said, "O Messenger of Allah! I intend to send abundant prayers upon you. How much should I do?" The Prophet ﷺ said, "As much as you like." Ubayy asked, "A quarter (of my supplications)?" The Prophet ﷺ said, "As much as you wish. But if you were to increase it, it would be better." Ubayy said, "A third?" The Prophet ﷺ said, "As much as you wish. But if you were to increase it, it would be better." Ubayy said, "Half?" The Prophet ﷺ said, "As much as you wish. But if you were to increase it, it would be better." Ubayy said, "Two thirds?" The Prophet ﷺ said, "As much as you wish. But if you were to increase it, it would be better." Ubayy said, "O Messenger of Allah! Then I will dedicate all my supplications to you." The Prophet ﷺ said, "Then you will be sufficed of all your needs and forgiven your sins."[25]

Abu Talhah said, "I entered upon the Prophet ﷺ and saw him in a state of elation and relaxedness that I had not seen before. So I asked him about it and he said, 'What

---

24 Aḥmad, Ibn Ḥibbān, and al-Ṭabarānī

25 Sunan al-Tirmidhī

would prevent me from that when Jibrīl came suddenly and brought me glad tidings from the Lord (Mighty and Majestic is He). Jibrīl said, "Allah (Exalted is he) sent me to give you glad tidings that no one from your Ummah will send prayers upon you except that Allah and His Angels will send ten prayers upon him.""""[26]

Jabir ibn Abdullah said, "The Prophet ﷺ said, 'If someone says, at the time of hearing the *adhān*, "O Allah! Lord of this perfect call and of the prayer that will be established! Grant Muhammad *al-wasīlah* and superiority and place him in the praiseworthy station that You have promised him," my intercession for him on the Day of Judgement will be obligatory.'"[27]

Sa'd ibn Abi Waqqas narrated that the Prophet ﷺ said, "If someone says, at the time of hearing the adhān, 'I bear witness that there is no god but Allah. He is one and without partner. And I bear witness that Muhammad is His slave and Messenger. I am satisfied with Allah as my Lord, with Muhammad as my Messenger, and with Islam as my religion,' he will be forgiven."[28]

Ibn Wahb narrated that the Prophet ﷺ said, "If someone sends peace upon me ten times, it is as if he has freed a slave."

In some traditional reports, the Prophet ﷺ is reported to have said, "Some people will come to me and I will

---

26 Sunan al-Nasā'ī; Saḥīḥ Ibn Ḥibbān; al-Bayhaqī

27 Saḥīḥ Bukhārī

28 Saḥīḥ Muslim

only recognize them through the copious prayers that they sent upon me." And in another report, he is reported to have said, "The safest of you on the Day of Judgement from its terrors and occurrences will be the one who has sent the most prayers upon me."[29]

Abu Bakr al-Siddiq is reported to have said, "Prayers upon the Prophet ﷺ are more effective against sins than cold water against fire. Sending peace upon him is better than freeing slaves."[30]

29 Al-Asbahānī, *al-Targhīb*

30 Al-Asbahānī, *al-Targhīb*

SECTION SIX

Censuring Those Who Do Not Send Prayers upon the Prophet ﷺ and the Sin That This Entails

Abu Hurairah said, "The Messenger of Allah ﷺ said, 'May he be made to regret in whose presence I am mentioned and he does not send prayers upon me. May he be made to regret upon whom Ramadan comes and goes and he is not forgiven. May he be made to regret whose parents reach old age in front of him and he does not enter Paradise through them both.'"[31] 'Abd al-Rahman said, "I think that he said, 'Or one of them (reach old age).'"

In another hadith, the Prophet ﷺ ascended the *minbar* and said, "*Āmīn.*" He ascended again and said "*Āmīn.*" He ascended a third time and said, "*Āmīn.*" Mu'adh asked the Prophet ﷺ about this and he responded, "Jibrīl came to me and said, 'O Muhammad! If you are mentioned in front of someone and they do not send prayers upon you, and he dies soon after, he will enter the Fire, for Allah will

---

31 Sunan al-Tirmidhī

have distanced him from Himself. Say, "Amin." So, I said, "Amin." Then he said the same for a person who reaches Ramadan and his fasting is not accepted of him, and he dies soon after. And he said the same for the one whose parents, or one of them, reaches old age and he does not treat them well, and dies soon after.[32]

'Ali ibn Abi Talib narrated that the Prophet ﷺ said, "The miser is the one in whose presence I am mentioned and he does not send prayers upon me."[33]

Ja'far ibn Muhammad narrated that his father said, "The Messenger of Allah ﷺ said, 'If I am mentioned in someone's presence and he does not send prayers upon me, he has deviated from the path to Paradise.'"[34]

'Ali ibn Abi Talib narrated that the Messenger of Allah ﷺ said, "The most miserly of all is the one in whose presence I am mentioned and he does not send prayers upon me."[35]

Abu Hurairah narrates that the Prophet ﷺ said, "If a group of people get together and then separate before they remember Allah and send prayers upon the Prophet ﷺ, they will be in a predicament before Allah. If He wills, He will punish them. And if He wills, He will forgive them."[36]

---

32 Al-Ḥākim

33 Sunan al-Tirmidhī; Sunan al-Nasā'ī; al-Bayhaqī

34 Al-Bayhaqī, *Shu'b al-Iman*

35 Al-Bukhārī in *al-Tārīkh*; Sunan al-Nasā'ī; al-Bayhaqī

36 Sunan Abū Dāwūd, Sunan al-Tirmidhī, al-Ḥākim

Abu Hurairah (may Allah be pleased with him) narrated, "If someone forgets to send prayers upon me, he has forgotten the way to Paradise."[37]

Qatadah narrated that the Prophet ﷺ said, "Part of disloyalty is that I am mentioned in front of a person, but he does not send prayers upon me."[38]

Jabir narrated that the Prophet ﷺ said, "No group of people sits together and then separates without sending prayers upon the Prophet ﷺ except that they separate with each having the rotten smell of disloyalty."[39]

Abu Sa'id narrated that the Prophet ﷺ said, "No people sit together without sending prayers upon the Prophet ﷺ except that they will regret it, even if they enter Paradise, because of the reward that they see that they have missed."[40]

Abu 'Isa al-Tirmidhī narrated from some of the people of knowledge that if a man sends prayers upon the Prophet ﷺ in a gathering, it will expiate for him any mistakes that occur in that gathering.

---

37 Al-Bayhaqī, *Shu'b al-Iman*

38 A narration from 'Abd al-Razzaq from Ma'amar. It is a *mursal* hadith that is used only for encouraging good works and not to establish rulings.

39 Al-Bayhaqī; al-Tayālīsī; al-Nasā'ī

40 Al-Bayhaqī

SECTION SEVEN

On His ﷺ Being Singled Out for Having the Prayer and Salutation Upon Him Delivered to Him

Abu Hurairah (may Allah be pleased with him) narrated that the Messenger of Allah ﷺ said, "No one will greet me with peace except that Allah will return to me my spirit so that I can return his greeting."[41]

Abu Bakr ibn Abi Shaybah mentioned that Abu Hurairah said, "The Messenger of Allah ﷺ said, 'If someone sends prayers upon me at my grave, I will hear him, and if he sends prayers upon me from afar, it will be conveyed to me.'"[42]

Ibn Mas'ud narrates that Allah has Angels that circulate the earth that convey to the Prophet ﷺ the greetings of his *Ummah*.[43] Abu Hurairah narrated something similar.

Ibn 'Umar is narrated to have said, "Send copious

---

41 Aḥmad; Sunan Abū Dāwūd; al-Bayhaqī

42 Al-Bayhaqī, *Shu'b al-Iman*

43 Aḥmad; Sunan al-Nasā'ī; Ibn Ḥibbān; al- Ḥākim; al-Bayhaqī in *Shu'b al-Iman*

greetings upon your Prophet every Jumu'ah, for he will be conveyed that from you every Jumu'ah." In one narration, the Prophet ﷺ said, "No one sends prayers upon me except that his prayer will be conveyed to me as soon as he finishes it."

Al-Hasan narrated that the Prophet ﷺ said, "Wherever you are, send prayers upon me, for your prayers will be conveyed to me."[44]

Ibn 'Abbas said, "No one from the *Ummah* of Muhammad ﷺ sends prayers upon him except that it is conveyed to him."

Some of the scholars mentioned that when a slave sends prayers upon the Prophet ﷺ, his name is conveyed to him (with his prayer).

Al-Hasan ibn 'Ali said that when one enters the *Masjid*, he should greet the Prophet ﷺ with peace. The Messenger of Allah ﷺ said, "Do not make visiting my grave into a festival, and do not make your houses into graves. Send prayers upon me wherever you are, for your prayer will be conveyed to me from wherever you are."[45]

In a hadith narrated by Aws, the Prophet ﷺ said, "Send copious prayers upon me on the Day of Jumu'ah. Your prayers will be presented to me."[46]

Sulayman ibn Suhaym said, "I saw the Prophet ﷺ in a dream. I said, 'O Messenger of Allah! Do you understand

---

44 Ibn Abī Shaybah; al-Ṭabarānī

45 Al-Ṭabarānī

46 Sunan Abū Dāwūd; Sunan al-Tirmidhī; Sunan al-Nasā'ī; Sunan Ibn Mājah

the greeting of those who come to you and greet you with peace?' He said, 'Yes. And I return their greeting.'"[47]

Ibn Shihab said, "It has reached us that the Messenger of Allah ﷺ said, "Send copious prayers upon me on the luminous night and the radiant day,[48] for they will be conveyed on your behalf. The earth does not consume the bodies of the prophets. No Muslim sends prayers upon me except that it is carried by an Angel until he conveys it to me. He will name the one who performed it, saying, 'So-and-so says such-and-such.'"[49]

47 Ibn Abī al-Dunyā; al-Bayhaqī

48 Meaning the night and day of Friday.

49 I.e. a *mursal* hadith.

SECTION EIGHT

Disagreement Over Sending Prayers Upon Other than the Prophet ﷺ and the Rest of the Prophets (peace be upon them)

Al-Qāḍī[50] (may Allah grant him success) said, "All the scholars are unanimous that it is permissible to send prayers upon the Prophet ﷺ." However, it has been narrated that Ibn 'Abbas said that it is not permissible to send prayers upon anyone other than the Prophet ﷺ. In another narration, he said that it is not permissible to send prayers upon anyone other than the prophets.

Sufyan said, "Sending prayers upon anyone other than a prophet is disliked. And I have found in the writing of one of my Sheikhs, "The school of Mālik deems it impermissible to send prayers upon any of the prophets besides Muhammad ﷺ." However, this is not the normative opinion in the school.

In *Al-Mabsūt*, Mālik said to Yahya ibn Ishaq, "I disliked sending prayers upon anyone other than the prophets. We

---

50 Qāḍī ʿIyād

should not go beyond that to which we have been commanded." Yahya ibn Yahya said, "I do not act upon this statement of his. There is issue with sending prayers upon all the prophets, or upon others." He used as evidence the hadith of Ibn 'Umar, in which he mentioned the Prophet ﷺ instructing people in how to send prayers upon him. In that hadith, he said, "... (and send prayers) upon his wives and family."

I have also found attributed to Abu 'Imran al-Qasi that dislike of sending prayers upon other than the Prophet ﷺ. This has been narrated from Ibn 'Abbas (may Allah be pleased with father and son). Abu 'Imran said, "That is our opinion." He would not send prayers upon anyone else.

It has also been narrated from 'Abd al-Razzaq that Abu Hurairah (may Allah be pleased with him) said, "The Messenger of Allah ﷺ said, 'Send prayers upon the prophets of Allah and His Messengers, for Allah sent them just as He sent me.'"[51]

The scholars have deemed that the chains of transmission from Ibn 'Abbas are not relied upon for establishing rulings. In addition, prayer (*ṣalāh*) in the language of the Arabs carries the meaning of showing compassion and supplication. This is unrestricted and permissible until an authentic hadith or consensus of the scholars establishes its interdiction. Furthermore, Allah (Exalted is He) said, "It is He who sends prayers upon you, and His Angels (also send prayers)" (*al-Aḥzāb*, 33:43). He (Exalted is He)

---

51 Aḥmad; al-Ṭabarānī

also said, "Take charity from their wealth. In that way, you will cleanse them and purify them. And pray upon them" (*al-Tawbah*, 9:103). The Prophet ﷺ said, "O Allah! Send prayers upon the family of Ubayy and the family of Awfa."[52] And whenever any people would come to him with charity, he would say, "O Allah! Send prayers upon so-and-so."

In the hadith of the prayer upon him, the Prophet ﷺ taught, "O, Allah! Send prayers upon Muhammad, his wives, and his offspring." In another version, he added, "And upon the family of Muhammad." It has been said that "his family" could refer to his followers, his *Ummah*, the people of his household, his followers, his clan, his tribe, his children, his people, or – in this specific case – to his people for whom taking charity was forbidden.

In one narration, Anas narrates that the Prophet ﷺ was asked, "Who is the family of Muhammad?" He said, "Every God-conscious person."

It has come in the school of al-Hasan al-Basrī that the meaning of *Āl Muhammad* is Muhammad himself, as the Prophet ﷺ would say in his prayers upon himself, "O Allah! Single out for Your prayers and blessings, the family of Muhammad." The Prophet ﷺ was referring to himself because he would not have left out that which Allah (Exalted is He) had commanded as an obligation, which is to send prayers upon Muhammad ﷺ himself.

---

52 Saḥīḥ Muslim; Saḥīḥ Bukhārī

That would be similar to his saying, "I have been given something similar to the flutes of the family of Dāwūd."[53] He meant the flutes of Dāwūd himself.

In another hadith of Abu Humayd al-Sa'idi, the prayer upon the Prophet ﷺ was mentioned as, "O Allah! Send prayers upon Muhammad, his wives, and his offspring." Ibn 'Umar narrates that he would send prayers upon the Prophet ﷺ, Abu Bakr, and 'Umar. Mālik narrated it in his *Muwaṭṭa'* from the narrations of Yahya al-Andalusi. However, the authentic narration from another transmitter is that he would supplicate for Abu Bakr and 'Umar.

Ibn Wahb narrated from Anas ibn Mālik, "We would supplicate for our Companions in their absence. We would say, "O Allah! Single so-and-so out for Your prayers which You send upon the righteous people who pray throughout the night and fast during the day." Al-Qāḍī 'Iyad said, "The researchers have nevertheless inclined towards and chosen the opinion of Mālik and Sufyan (may Allah have mercy on both)."[54]

However, an opinion that was narrated from Ibn 'Abbas and preferred by many of the jurists and theologians is that it is unlawful to send prayers upon non-prophets when they are mentioned. They opined that it is something for which the prophets were chosen to display respect and veneration. It is similar to Allah being singled out for declaring His transcendence, holiness, and great-

---

53 Saḥīḥ Bukhārī; Saḥīḥ Muslim

54 That sending prayers upon people who are not prophets is disliked.

ness. This is something that is not done for anyone else. Thus, in the same way, it is obligatory to restrict sending prayers and salutations to the Prophet ﷺ and all the other prophets. It should not be done for anyone else, just as Allah ordered in His words, "Send prayers upon him and extend him a worthy salutation" (*al-Aḥzāb*, 33:56). Others, such as the Imams and scholars, should only be extended prayers for Divine forgiveness and satisfaction, as in His (Exalted is He) words, "They say: Our Lord! Forgive us and our brethren who preceded us in faith" (*al-Ḥashr*, 59:10). He also said, "And those who followed them in good, Allah was pleased with them" (*al-Tawbah*, 9:100).

Likewise, it was not well-known in the first generations, just as Abu 'Imran said. Rather, it is something that the *Rāfidah* and Shia invented. They extended the duty to send prayers to the mention of some of the Imams, making them like the Prophet ﷺ in that regard. Since it is obligatory to avoid semblance with the people of heretical innovations, it is therefore necessary to oppose them in what they have necessitated of that. Mentioning prayers upon the family and the wives, along with the Prophet ﷺ, is from the standpoint of their following and being connected to him, not because of any election they have in and of themselves.

The scholars who transmit this opinion say, "The prayer upon the Prophet ﷺ upon those who he sent prayers upon is interpreted as supplication and turning towards them. It is not in the meaning of respect and veneration." They also said, "Allah (Exalted is he) has said, 'Do not make your calling of the Messenger similar to your calling of one another' (*al-Nūr*, 24:63)." Likewise, it is necessary that one's supplication for him be different to the supplication for other people. This is the preference of Abu Muzaffar al-Isfarayini, one of our Sheikhs, and it was echoed by Abu 'Umar ibn 'Abd al-Barr.

SECTION NINE

On the Ruling on Visiting Him, the Excellence of Those Who Visit Him and Greet Him With Peace, and the Method of That Greeting

Visiting the Prophet ﷺ is one of the practices of the Muslims that has been agreed upon. It is an excellent practice that is encouraged. Ibn 'Umar (may Allah be pleased with father and son) said, "The Prophet ﷺ said, 'If someone visits my grave, my intercession will be obligatory for him.'"[55]

Anas ibn Mālik said, "The Messenger of Allah ﷺ said, 'If someone visits me in Madinah, hoping for a reward, he will be one of my neighbours, and I will be an intercessor for him on the Day of Judgement.'"[56]

In another Hadith, he said, "If someone visits me after my death, it is as if he has visited me during my life."[57]

---

55 Saḥīḥ Ibn Khuzaymah

56 Al-Bayhaqī

57 Al-Bayhaqī

However, Mālik disliked this, saying, "We visited the grave of the Prophet ﷺ, but people differed over the reason for that. It has been said that it is a dislike for the term itself because of what has been narrated, that the Prophet ﷺ said, 'Allah has cursed the visitors of graves.'[58] However, that is contradicted by his words, "I used to forbid your visiting graves. However, now (I tell you) to visit them,"[59] and his words, 'If someone visits my grave'[60] because he has used the term ('grave')."

It has also been said that the visitor is better than the visited. However, this is also baseless, because not every visitor is described as such. This is not a universal rule. It has been narrated in another hadith that the people of Paradise will visit their Lord. If this saying were true, then it would not be appropriate to use these terms with regards to Him (Exalted is He).

Abu 'Imaran (may Allah have mercy on him) said, "Mālik disliked that one say '*Tawāf al-Ziyarah* (the *Tawāf* of visitation)' and 'We visited the grave of the Prophet ﷺ' because it is a phrase that is used between people. He disliked the possibility of people putting others on the same level as the Prophet ﷺ through that expression. Rather, he preferred for people to say specifically for the Prophet ﷺ, 'We are greeting the Prophet ﷺ.' Furthermore, visiting people is something only permissible, while it is a

---

58 Aḥmad; Sunan al-Tirmidhī; Saḥīḥ Ibn Ḥibbān

59 Saḥīḥ Muslim

60 Ibn Khuzaymah

requirement to make every effort to visit the grave of the Prophet ﷺ."

What he meant by requirement was a firm recommendation, encouragement, and emphasis, not necessarily an obligation. However, in my own judgment, the most likely reason is that the Mālik's dislike was because of its being ascribed to the grave of the Prophet ﷺ. If the expression were 'We visited the Prophet ﷺ' he would not have disliked it, due to the saying of the Prophet ﷺ, "O Allah! Do not make my grave an idol that is worshiped after me. The wrath of Allah is intense over people who took the graves of their prophets as mosques."[61] So, he removed the ascription of that expression to the grave, along with any resemblance to the actions of those, by cutting off the means and locking the door. And Allah knows best.

The jurist Ishaq ibn Ibrahim said, "Among those things that continue to be practiced by those who perform Hajj is to pass through Madinah with the objective of praying in the *Masjid* of the Messenger of Allah ﷺ and to take blessings from seeing his *rawdah*[62], his *minbar*, his grave, the places he sat, the things he touched, the places his feet passed, the wall he used to lean upon, where Jibrīl would descend with revelation, and through those who frequented there and visited it among the Companions and the Muslim Imams. All of this is recommended.

---

61 Al-Muwaṭṭa'

62 The area between his grave and his *minbar*.

Ibn Abi Fudayk said, "I have heard someone I met[63] saying, 'We have been informed that if someone stands in front of the grave of the Prophet ﷺ and recites the verse, "Allah and His Angels send prayers upon the Prophet..." and then says, "May Allah send prayers upon you, O Muhammad" seventy times, that an Angel will call him, saying, "May Allah send prayers upon you, so-and-so," and he will not leave any of his needs unfulfilled.'"

Yazid ibn Abi Sa'id al-Mahri said, "I came to 'Umar ibn 'Abd al-'Aziz, and when I wanted to bid him farewell, he said, 'I need something from you. When you reach Madinah, you will see the grave of the Prophet ﷺ. Greet him on my behalf.'" Someone else said that 'Umar ibn 'Abd al-'Aziz would travel from the Levant to Madinah just to greet the Prophet ﷺ.

One of the scholars said, "I saw Anas ibn Mālik come to the grave of the Prophet ﷺ. He stood in front of it and raised his hands until I thought that he was going to begin to pray. Then, he greeted the Prophet ﷺ and departed."

According to the narration of Ibn Wahb, Mālik said that when someone greets the Prophet ﷺ, he should supplicate standing and facing the grave, not the *qiblah*. He should then come close (to the grave) and greet him with peace, but he should not touch the grave. However, in *Al-Mabsūt*, he is reported to have said, "I do not accept that someone stands in front of the grave of the Prophet ﷺ and supplicates. Rather, he should greet him and then leave."

---

63 I.e. a scholar.

Ibn Abi Mālikiyyah said, "If someone wishes to stand facing the Prophet ﷺ, then let him stand in the direction of the *qiblah* by the grave."

Nafi' said, "Ibn 'Umar would greet the Prophet ﷺ at his grave. I saw him come to the grave more than a hundred times and say, 'Peace be upon the Prophet ﷺ. Peace be upon Abu Bakr. Peace be upon my father.' Then he would depart."

Ibn 'Umar was seen placing his hand on the place where the Prophet ﷺ would sit on the *minbar* and then wiping it on his face.

Ibn Qusayt and al-'Utbi both said, "When the *Masjid* emptied out, the Companions of the Prophet ﷺ would rub their right hands over the knob of the *minbar* that faced the grave and then turn towards the *qiblah* and supplicate."

In the *Muwaṭṭa'*, Yahya ibn al-Layth narrated that Ibn 'Umar would stand at the grave of the Prophet ﷺ and send prayers upon the Prophet, Abu Bakr, and 'Umar. However, in the narrations of Ibn al-Qasim and al-Qa'nabi, he would only supplicate for Abu Bakr and 'Umar.

In the narration of Ibn Wahb, Mālik said that the one who is greeting the Prophet ﷺ should say, "May the peace, mercy and blessings of Allah be upon you, O Prophet." In *Al-Mabsūt*, he is narrated to have said that one should also greet Abu Bakr and 'Umar.

Qāḍī Abu al-Walid al-Baji said, "In my opinion, one should supplicate for the Prophet ﷺ with the expression of prayer and then supplicate for Abu Bakr and 'Umar, just as in the Hadith of Ibn 'Umar that was mentioned."

Ibn Habīb said:

When someone enters the *Masjid* of the Messenger of Allah ﷺ, he should say, "In the Name of Allah. Peace be upon the Messenger of Allah. Peace be upon us from our Lord. May Allah and His Angels send prayers upon Muhammad. O Allah! Forgive me my sins and open for me the doors of Your mercy and Paradise. Protect me from Satan the accursed." Then he should head to the *rawdah*, which is between the grave and the *minbar*. There, he should pray two *rak'ahs* before standing before the grave. He should praise Allah in both of them and ask Allah to grant all his objectives and help him achieve them. If he prays in the *Masjid* at a place other than the *rawdah*, it will suffice. However, praying in the *rawdah* is superior. The Prophet ﷺ said, "The area between my house and my *minbar* is one of the gardens of Paradise." And he has said, "My *minbar* is upon one of the gardens of Paradise." Then he should stand at the grave, humbling himself and showing veneration. He should send prayers upon him and extol him with whatever words come to him. Then he greets Abu Bakr and 'Umar and prays for them both. One should pray as much as one is able in the *Masjid* of the Prophet ﷺ, day and night. He should not leave out praying in *Masjid Qubā'* or the graves of the martyrs.

As related in the book of Muhammad ﷺ,[64] Mālik said, "He should greet the Prophet ﷺ whenever he enters or

64 The *Sharh*. Mulla 'Ali al-Qari states that this refers to one of the companions of Mālik and may in fact be Muhammad ibn al-Hasan al-Shaybani, the companion of Abu Hanifah.

exits Madinah and while he is there." Muhammad ﷺ said, "And when he is leaving, he should make the final act he performs his standing at the grave. This is the same if someone leaves on a journey from Madinah."[65]

Ibn Wahb narrated that Fatimah bint Muhammad narrated that the Prophet ﷺ said, "When you enter the *Masjid*, send prayers upon the Prophet ﷺ. Then say, 'O Allah! Forgive me my sins. And open for me the doors to Your Mercy.' And when you leave, send prayers upon the Prophet ﷺ. Then say, 'O Allah! Forgive me my sins. And open for me the doors to Your grace.'"[66]

In another narration, he said, "Greet" instead of "Send prayers." He also added that, when exiting, he should say, "O Allah! I ask You to grant me something of Your grace."[67]

Muhammad ibn Sirin said, "When people used to enter the *Masjid* (of the Prophet ﷺ), they would say, 'May Allah and His Angels end prayers upon Muhammad. Peace be upon you, O Prophet, and the mercy and blessings of Allah. In the Name of Allah, we enter. And in the name of Allah, we exit.' And they would say something similar when exiting."

It is also narrated on the authority of Fatimah that when the Prophet ﷺ would enter the *Masjid*, he would say, "May Allah send prayers and peace upon Muhammad." Then, in the same narration, she mentioned some-

---

65 I.e. that person should visit the Prophet ﷺ when he leaves and returns.

66 Sunan Abū Dāwūd; Sunan al-Nasā'ī; Sunan al-Tirmidhī; Sunan Ibn Mājah

67 Sunan Abū Dāwūd

thing similar to the previous hadith. In another version, he praised Allah, invoked His name, and sent prayers upon himself. The rest of the hadith is the same. In another narration, he would say, "In the Name of Allah. Peace be upon the Messenger of Allah ﷺ."

Another Companion narrated that, when entering the *Masjid*, the Messenger of Allah ﷺ would say, "O Allah! Open for me the doors of Your mercy, and facilitate for me the doors to Your sustenance."

Abu Hurairah said, "When one of you enters the *Masjid*, he should send prayers upon the Prophet ﷺ and say, 'O, Allah! Open for me the doors of Your mercy.'"[68]

Mālik said, as reported in *Al-Mabsūt*, "It is not necessary for the residents of Madinah to stand at the grave when they enter or exit the *Masjid*. That is only for the travellers." He also said, in the same text, "However, there is no problem if one who is returning from a journey, or setting out, to stand at the grave of the Prophet ﷺ, and then send prayers upon him and supplicate for him, Abu Bakr and 'Umar." It was said to him, "Some people from the residents of Madinah, who are neither returning from a journey nor intending one, do this once or more a day. And perhaps they stand at the grave on Jumu'ah or during other blessed days once, twice, or more, greeting the Prophet ﷺ and supplicating for an hour." He replied, "That has not been conveyed to us from anyone among the jurists of our land, so leaving it is better. The last of

68 Saḥīḥ Ibn Ḥibbān; Saḥīḥ Ibn Khuzaymah

this *Ummah* will only be rectified by that which rectified its predecessors. It has not reached me regarding the predecessors and its early people that they would do that. It is disliked, except for someone who returns from a journey or intends one."

Ibn al-Qasim said, "I saw that the people of Madinah would, when leaving on a journey or returning from one, go to the grave and greet the Prophet ﷺ. And that is my opinion (i.e. practice)."

Al-Baji said, "The difference between the people of Madinah and the visitors is that the visitors only came to Madinah for that, while the residents of Madinah live there and did not come only for the sake of visiting the grave and greeting the Prophet ﷺ. The Prophet ﷺ said, 'O, Allah! Do not make my grave into an idol that is worshiped. The wrath of Allah is intense over those who made the graves of their prophets into mosques.' He also said, 'Do not make (visiting) my grave into a festival.'"

Regarding those who stand by the grave, Ahmad ibn Sa'id al-Hindi stated in his book, "They should not cling to it, nor should they touch it or stand there for a long time."

In *Al-'Utbiyyah*, it is stated that in *Masjid* al-Nabi, one first prays before greeting the Prophet ﷺ. The most preferred place is the prayer area of the Prophet ﷺ, next to the incense burner. The best place for the obligatory prayer is wherever he ends up in the rows. For the travellers, it is preferred that they make their voluntary prayers in it rather than in one of the houses (of Madinah).

SECTION TEN

On the Etiquette of Entering the Noble Prophetic *Masjid*, Its Excellence and the Excellence of Madinah and Makkah

This section is on the etiquette that is required of the person who enters the *Masjid* of the Prophet ﷺ in addition to what we have already mentioned, i.e. on the excellence of the *Masjid*; on the excellence of praying in it; on the excellence of the *Masjid* of Makkah; a description of the grave and *minbar* of the Prophet ﷺ; and on the excellence of the residents of Madinah and Makkah.

Allah (Exalted is He) said, "A *Masjid* that was established upon God-consciousness from day one is more appropriate for you to stand therein" (*al-Tawbah*, 9:108).

It has been narrated that the Prophet ﷺ was asked which *Masjid* this referred to. He responded, "My *Masjid*."[69] This is the opinion of Ibn al-Musayyab, Zayd ibn Thabit, Ibn 'Umar, Mālik ibn Anas and others. However, Ibn 'Abbas is reported to have the opinion that it refers to *Masjid Qubā'*.

---

69 Ṣaḥīḥ Muslim

Abu Hurairah (may Allah be pleased with him) narrated that the Prophet ﷺ said, "No one should set out to visit any *Masjid* except three: *al-Masjid al-Harām*, my *Masjid*, or *Masjid al-Aqsa*."[70]

We have already mentioned the narrations regarding sending prayers and peace upon the Prophet ﷺ when one enters the *Masjid*.

Abdullah ibn 'Amr ibn al-'As narrated that when the Prophet ﷺ would enter the *Masjid*, he would say, "I seek refuge in Allah, the Immensely Great, in His Noble Countenance and in His Eternal Dominion, from the accursed Satan."[71]

Mālik (may Allah have mercy on him) said, "'Umar ibn al-Khattab heard a loud voice in the *Masjid*. He called the person over and said, 'Where are you from?' The man replied, 'I am a man from *Thaqīf*.' 'Umar said, 'If you had been from these two towns, I would have disciplined you.' We do not raise our voices in this *Masjid* of ours.'"

Muhammad ibn Maslamah said, "It is not fitting for anyone to enter or stay in the *Masjid* raising his voice, or to do anything uncouth or harmful within. He should avoid anything disliked while in the *Masjid*."

Al-Qāḍī 'Iyad says, "All of this has been mentioned by Qāḍī Isma'il in *Al-Mabsūt*, in the chapter on the excellence of the *Masjid* of the Prophet ﷺ. However, all the scholars are in agreement that these are the rules of all *Masjids*."

---

70 Saḥīḥ Bukhārī; Saḥīḥ Muslim; Sunan al-Nasā'ī; Sunan Abū Dāwūd

71 Sunan Abū Dāwūd

Qāḍī Isma'il also says, "Muhammad ibn Maslamah said, 'In the *Masjid* of the Messenger of Allah ﷺ it is disliked for those praying to raise their voices to such an extent that they may interrupt each other's prayers. One is not to raise his voice in any of the acts that are specific to that *Masjid*. In fact, raising one's voice in *talbiyah*[72] is disliked in all mosques where *Jumu'ah* is performed, except *al-Masjid al-Harām* and our *Masjid*.'"[73]

Abu Hurairah narrated that the Prophet ﷺ said, "A prayer in my *Masjid* is better than one thousand prayers in any other *Masjid*, except *al-Masjid al-Harām*."[74]

Al-Qāḍī 'Iyad) says: "People differed over the meaning of this exception along the lines of their differing over whether Makkah or Madinah is superior. Mālik was, according to the narration of Ashhab, of the opinion, along with Ibn Nafi' - his companion - and a group of his companions, that the meaning of the hadith is that a prayer in the *Masjid* of the Prophet ﷺ is still superior to praying in *al-Masjid al-Harām*, but only superior to a smaller number of prayers than one thousand. Their proof is that it has been narrated that 'Umar ibn al-Khattab said, "A prayer in *al-Masjid al-Harām* is better than one hundred prayers

---

72 That is "Labbayk Allahumma..." The invocation of the pilgrims who have entered the state of *ihram*.

73 There is a discrepancy in the text. Mulla 'Ali al-Qari states that "our *Masjid*" is either something that was inadvertently added to the text, or that the original wording was "*Masjid* Mina." Otherwise, *talbiyah* is not performed in the *Masjid* of the Prophet or anywhere else apart from the *Haram* and Mina. (Summarized from *Sharh Al-Shifā li al-Qāḍī* 'Iyād, Mullah 'Ali al-Qari).

74 Saḥīḥ al-Bukhārī; Saḥīḥ Muslim

in any other *Masjid*."[75] Thus, those one hundred prayers would leave the *Masjid* of the Messenger of Allah ﷺ at 900 prayers in *al-Masjid al-Harām*, and better than one thousand in other mosques. This opinion is built upon the opinion that Madinah is superior to Makkah, as we have said. This is the opinion of 'Umar ibn al-Khattab, Mālik and the majority of the people of Madinah.

The people of Makkah and Kufa were of the opinion that Makkah is superior. That is the opinion of 'Ata', Ibn Wahb, Ibn Habīb and the companions of Mālik. Al-Saji also reported this as the opinion of al-Shāfi'ī. Those who had this opinion interpreted the exclusion in the aforementioned hadith as literal. According to them, a prayer in *al-Masjid al-Harām* is superior. Their evidence for that is the hadith of Abdullah ibn al-Zubayr that has the same wording as the hadith of Abu Hurairah, with the addition of, "And a prayer in *al-Masjid al-Harām* is better than one hundred prayers in my *Masjid*."[76] Qatada narrated something similar. Thus, according to this, a prayer in *al-Masjid al-Harām* would be better than one hundred thousand prayers in all other mosques.

However, there is no disagreement over the fact that his grave is the best piece of land on earth. Qāḍī Abu al-

---

75 Mulla 'Ali al-Qari states that this an aberrant narration. The correct wording that has been narrated through a number of different chains of transmission is as follows: "A prayer in *al-Masjid al-Haram* is better than one thousand prayers in any other *masjid*, except the *masjid* of the Messenger of Allah ﷺ. A prayer in *al-Masjid al-Harām* is superior to one hundred prayers in his *Masjid*."

76 Aḥmad; Ibn Ḥibbān

Walid al-Baji said, "The hadith (of Abu Hurairah) in reality establishes the superiority of the *Masjid* of Makkah over all other *Masjids*. However, its superiority in relation to Madinah is not known from the hadith."

Al-Tahawi opined that such a superiority (of the two *Masjids* over other *Masjids*) would only concern the obligatory prayers. Mutawwaf, one of our companions, on the other hand, stated that it includes voluntary prayers. He also said, "Jumu'ah in them (the two *Masjids*) is better than Jumu'ah in the rest, and Ramadan in them is better than Ramadan in the rest."

'Abd al-Razzaq narrated a similar hadith to prove the superiority of Ramadan in Madinah over other cities.[77]

The Prophet ﷺ said, "That which is between my house and my *minbar* is one of the Gardens of Paradise."[78] Something similar has been narrated from Abu Hurairah and Abu Sa'id. The latter added, "My *minbar* is over my pond (*hawd*)."[79] In another hadith, the Prophet ﷺ said, "My *minbar* is upon one of the gardens of Paradise."

Al-Tabari said:

> There are two possible meanings. The first is that the meaning of 'house' here is the house in which he lived, considering that there is another narration that clarifies

---

77 The Hadith mentioned is on the authority of Bilal ibn al-Harith, that Ramadan and Jumu'ah in Madinah are better than in other places. It was narrated by al-Ṭabarānī.

78 Saḥīḥ al-Bukhārī; Saḥīḥ Muslim

79 Al-Muwaṭṭa'

> this: "What is between my apartment and my *minbar*…" The second is that the meaning of 'house' is his grave. This is the opinion of Zayd ibn Aslam on this hadith. It has also been narrated, "…what is between my grave and my *minbar*…' Since his grave is in his house, the meanings of the different narrations are in agreement, with no contradiction between them. That is because his grave is in his apartment, which is his house.

Al-Baji said:

> His words "my *minbar* is upon my pond" have a number of different possible interpretations. One of them is that it means that his actual *minbar*, which he had in this world, will be at his pond. This is the most plausible meaning. The second is that he will have a *minbar* there. The third meaning of his *minbar* and its presence with him at the pond is that through adhering to good deeds, one will arrive at the pond and be given to drink therefrom.

Al-Dāwūdi said, "His words 'one of the Gardens of Paradise' have two possible meanings. The first is that it is a cause for that. In other words, supplication and prayer in that area merit Paradise as a reward, just as it is said, "Paradise lies under the shade of swords."[80] The second possible meaning is that Allah will transfer that piece of earth itself and place it in Paradise."

---

80 Saḥīḥ al-Bukhārī; Saḥīḥ Muslim

Ibn 'Umar and a group of the Companions narrated that the Prophet ﷺ said, "No one bears the affliction and difficulty of Madinah patiently except that I will be a witness and an intercessor for him on the Day of Judgement."[81] He said about those who leave Madinah (to reside somewhere else), "Madinah is better for them, if they only knew."[82]

He also said, "Madinah is like a bellow. It removes the impurities (of metal) and leaves the pure substance."[83]

He also said, "No one leaves Madinah desiring to settle someplace else except that Allah replaces him with someone better."[84]

It is narrated that he said, "If someone dies in one of the two *Harams* (sanctuaries) while performing Hajj or 'Umrah, Allah will resurrect him on the Day of Judgement, and he will not have any judgement or punishment."[85] In another narration of the same hadith, he said, "... he will be resurrected among those who are saved on the Day of Judgement."[86]

Ibn 'Umar narrates that the Prophet ﷺ said, "If someone is able, let him die in Madinah, for I will intercede for anyone who dies therein."[87]

---

81 Saḥīḥ Muslim

82 Saḥīḥ al-Bukhārī; Saḥīḥ Muslim

83 Saḥīḥ al-Bukhārī; Saḥīḥ Muslim

84 Saḥīḥ Muslim

85 Al-Bayhaqī; al-Dāraquṭnī

86 Al-Bayhaqī; al-Ṭabarānī

87 Sunan Ibn Mājah; Sunan al-Tirmidhī; Saḥīḥ Ibn Ḥibbān

Allah (Exalted is He) said, "Indeed, the first house that was built for mankind is the one at *Bakkah*, blessed and a guidance for people. In it are evident signs, the *Maqām* of Ibrahim. Whoever enters it is safe" (*Āl ʿImrān*, 3:96–97).

Some of the scholars of *tafsīr* have said that the meaning of "safe" is "safe from the Fire." It has also been said it means that, during the time of Jāhiliyyah, whoever did an objectionable act outside of the *Haram* and then fled to it was safe from retribution. According to some opinions, it is similar to His words, "When We made the House a place of return for people and a sanctuary" (*al-Baqarah*, 2:125).

It is narrated that some people came to Sa'dun al-Khalwani in Munastir. They informed him that Kutamah intended to kill a man. They roasted him in a fire for an entire night, but it had no effect on him. His skin remained white. Sa'dun said, "Has he, perhaps, performed Hajj three times?" They said, "Yes." He said, "It has been narrated to me, as a hadith, that if someone performs Hajj once, he has fulfilled his obligation. If he performs Hajj twice, he has loaned to his Lord (a beautiful loan). And if he performs Hajj three times, Allah will make his hair and flesh unlawful for Fire."

When the Messenger of Allah ﷺ saw the Ka'bah, he said, "Greetings to you, O House! How great a house you are! How great is your sanctity!"[88]

In another hadith, he is reported to have said, "No one supplicates to Allah (Exalted is He) at the black corner

88 Al-Ṭabarānī in *al-Awsaṭ*

[where the black stone is placed] or at the water spout except that Allah will grant him his request."[89]

He also said, "If someone prays two *rak'ahs* near the *Maqām*, his past and future sins will be forgiven, and he will be raised on the Day of Judgement among those who are safe."[90]

Ibn 'Abbas said, "I heard the Messenger of Allah ﷺ say, 'No one supplicates at this *multazam* except that Allah grants him his request.'[91] Ibn 'Abbas then said, "Since I heard that from the Messenger of Allah ﷺ, I have not supplicated Allah for anything at this *multazam* except that I was granted my request." 'Amr ibn Dinar said, "Since I heard that from Ibn 'Abbas, I have not supplicated Allah for anything at the *multazam* except that I was granted my request." Sufyan also said, "Since hearing that from 'Amr, I have not supplicated Allah for anything at the *multazam* except that I was granted my request." Al-Humaydi said, "Since hearing that from Sufyan, I have not supplicated Allah for anything at the *multazam* except that I was granted my request. Muhammad ibn Idris said, "Since I heard this from al-Humaydi, I have not supplicated Allah for anything at the *multazam* except that I was granted my request." Abu al-Hasan Muhammad ibn al-Hasan said, "Since hearing this from Muhammad ibn Idris, I have not supplicated Allah for anything at the *multazam* except that I was granted my request."

---

89 A *mursal* hadith related by al-Hasan al-Basrī (Mulla 'Ali al-Qari).

90 Al-Daylamī

91 Qāḍī 'Iyād narrates this hadith with his chain of transmission. He then mentions the comment of each of the narrators in his chain.

Abu Usamah said, "I do not remember if al-Hasan ibn Rashiq said anything about his supplications at the *multazam*. However, since I heard this hadith from al-Hasan ibn Rashiq, I have not supplicated Allah for anything at the *multazam* except that I was granted my request from this world. And I sincerely hope that my requests regarding the Hereafter have been granted." Al-'Udhri said, "Nor have I asked Allah for anything at the *multazam*, since hearing this hadith from Abu Usamah, except that I was granted my request." Abu 'Ali[92] said, "I have asked Allah for many things (at the *multazam*). Some of those requests have been granted. And I hope, of His vast bounty, that He grants me the rest."

Qāḍī Abu al-Fadl (Qāḍī 'Iyad) says, "We have mentioned a good portion of these traditions in this section, even though they do not technically belong to this chapter, because of their connection with the previous section. We did so hoping to complete its benefit. And Allah alone facilitates, out of His mercy, to that which is correct.

---

92 The student of al-'Udhri and the Sheikh of Qāḍī 'Iyād.

APPENDIX

Insights into Sending Prayers Upon the Prophet ﷺ

Ḥabīb ʿUmar bin Hafīẓ (may Allah protect him and benefit us through him) provides some valuable insights into sending prayers upon the Prophet ﷺ. Extracts from a lesson during the Dawah Conference, Dar al-Mustafa, Muharram 1433 / December 2011.

The Reality of Sending Prayers Upon Him ﷺ

Allah ordered us to send prayers upon the Prophet ﷺ but we are certain that we are unable to do anything of our own accord, so instead of attempting to do so we request that Allah Himself bestows prayers on the Prophet ﷺ. He called this request of ours prayers from us and said: Send prayers and peace upon him in abundance. (Al-Ahzab, 33:56) In reality, however, these prayers are from Him as we are incapable of sending them ourselves. That is why if we wish to send prayers upon the Prophet ﷺ we say 'O Allah,' or 'O Lord, send prayers upon him.'

If all your good actions were placed on one side of the scale and one prayer from Allah was placed on the other, the prayer from Allah would outweigh them all. Your actions cannot be compared to the actions of the Lord of the Worlds. In fact were not only your actions, but all the good actions of the whole of creation from the time of Adam to the Day of Judgment placed on one side of the scale and one prayer from the Lord of the Worlds was placed on the other, the prayer from Allah would outweigh all those actions. This is one prayer so what about ten prayers that Allah bestows in exchange for one prayer upon the Prophet Muhammad ﷺ?

How to Send Prayers Upon Him and Their Effect

Sending prayers upon the Prophet ﷺ strengthens your connection with Allah and His Messenger ﷺ since in doing so you are remembering both Allah and His Messenger ﷺ. This is especially true if you do it in a state of intense love, longing and veneration. You should be aware while doing so that the source of every blessing which Allah has bestowed upon you and the whole of creation, is Muhammad ﷺ and that his sublime light was the beginning point of creation. In addition, try to picture him ﷺ in front of you while you send prayers upon him ﷺ (especially if you have seen him previously) or picture your shaykh or his blessed Masjid or his Rawdah or his Shubbak (the screen in front of his blessed grave). Send prayers upon him as if you were there until the door is opened to you and the veil is lifted.

If you send prayers upon him in this state it will bring limitless benefits and will bear fruits that none of your actions could bring. It will be a means of purification and will assist you in your journey to Allah. If you do not have a shaykh, it will be a cause of you being united with him; if you already have a shaykh, it will strengthen your spiritual connection to him so that the door to the Prophet ﷺ can be opened more swiftly.

The hadith of Ubbay bin Ka'b [mentioned earlier in the translator's introduction] is sufficient evidence of the benefits of sending prayers upon the Prophet ﷺ.

If someone's worries have been removed and his sins have been forgiven then he has attained felicity in this life and the next. May Allah remove our worries and forgive our sins through His Beloved, the healer of our hearts.

The Relationship Between Sending Prayers Upon The Prophet and Calling to Allah

We must allot a portion of time in which we send prayers upon the Chosen One ﷺ. No one can be a caller to Allah if they do not spend some time sending prayers upon the one who first called to Allah and guided people to Him. In reality, no-one calls to Allah except as a representative and deputy of him ﷺ.

When someone sends prayers upon the Prophet ﷺ and then calls people to Allah, a light emanates from his mouth which reaches the people that are listening. The people are thus affected directly by the Prophet ﷺ and by the light of the prayers, not by the speaker himself. Thus, if someone sends abundant prayers upon the Prophet ﷺ and then calls people to Allah his words have a great effect on those he is calling.

Those calling to Allah have received many openings after repeating the prayer which Sayyiduna Muhammad al-Bakri and others received from the Prophet ﷺ:

اللّٰهُمَّ صَلِّ وسَلِّمْ وبَارِكْ على سَيِّدِنا مُحَمَّدٍ الفَاتِحِ لِمَا أُغْلِقَ الخَاتِمِ لِمَا سَبَقَ نَاصِرِ الحَقِّ بِالحَقِّ وَالهادِي إلى صِراطِكَ المُسْتَقِيمِ صلى اللهُ عَلَيْهِ وعلى آلِهِ وَصَحْبِهِ حَقَّ قَدْرِهِ وَمِقْدَارِهِ العَظِيم

Allah inspired in the Companions, those that came after them and the knowers of Allah, amazing prayers upon the Prophet ﷺ which greatly effect and illuminate the one reading them. You should read a portion of these prayers regularly because they are prayers that emanated from those who are in his presence ﷺ. Those who composed them or received them have knowledge of him which cannot be described and which you cannot come close to. If you pray with the prayers that emanated from their hearts you will receive precious gifts from them. It will be a cause for you to be swiftly brought close and to reach lofty stations. O Allah, do not deprive us of all the goodness that You possess because of the evil that we possess!

To illustrate the point, Ḥabīb ʻUmar then read two of Ḥabīb ʻAli al-Habashi's prayers:

اللّٰهُمَّ صَلِّ وَسَلِّمْ عَلَى سَيِّدِنَا مُحَمَّدٍ مِفْتَاحِ بَابِ رَحْمَةِ اللهِ ، عَدَدَ مَا فِي عِلْمِ اللهِ صَلاةً وَسَلامًا دائِمَيْنِ بِدَوَامِ مُلْكِ اللهِ ، وَعَلَى آلِهِ وَصَحْبِهِ وَسَلِّمْ

اللّٰهُمَّ صَلِّ وَسَلِّمْ وَبَارِكْ على سَيِّدِنا مُحَمَّدٍ أَوَّلِ مُتَلَقٍّ لِفَيْضِكَ الأَوَّل، وأَكْرَمِ حَبِيبٍ تَفَضَّلْتَ عَلَيْهِ فَتَفَضَّلَ وعلى آلِهِ وَصَحْبِهِ وَتَابِعِيهِ وَحِزْبِهِ ما دَامَ تَلَقِّيهِ مِنْكَ

وَتَرَقِّيهِ إِلَيْكَ وَ إِقْبالُكَ عَلَيْهِ وَإِقْبَالُهُ عَلَيْكَ وَشُهُودُهُ لَكَ وانْطِراحُهُ لَدَيْكَ صَلاةً نَشْهَدُكَ بِها مِنْ مِرَآتِهِ وَنَصِلُ بِها إلى حَضْرَتِكَ مِنْ حَضْرَةِ ذاتِهِ قائِمِينَ لَكَ وَلَهُ بِالأَدَبِ الوَافِرِ مَغْمُورِينَ مِنْكَ ومِنْهُ بِالمَدِدِ البَاطِنِ وَالظَّاهِرِ

Shaykh Yusuf bin Isma'il al-Nabahani collected many of the prayers of the Knowers of Allah. They can be found in Afḍal al-Salawāt and Sa'ādat al-Dārayn.

May Allah benefit us by sending prayers upon His Beloved.

Translation of the Three Prayers Mentioned

1. Allah, send Your prayers and peace upon our Master Muhammad, the one who opens that which is closed, the seal of those that came before, the defender of truth with truth and the guide to Your straight path (and upon his Family and Companions), in accordance with the greatness of his rank.
2. Allah, send Your prayers and peace upon our Master Muḥamad, the key to the door of the mercy of Allah, prayers and peace as numerous as that which the knowledge of Allah encompasses, remaining as long as the dominion of Allah remains, and upon his Family and Companions.
3. Allah, send Your prayers, peace and blessings upon our Master Muhammad, the foremost receiver of your first outpouring, the most noble beloved, upon whom You have bestowed Your favour and he thus excelled; and upon his Family, Companions, his

followers and those loyal to him, [prayers, peace and blessings] lasting as long as his receiving from You and his ascent towards You, and Your approach to him and his approach to You, and his witnessing of You and his humble prostration before You. By this prayer we shall witness You through his mirror and enter into Your presence through his presence, displaying to You and him the best etiquette, fully enveloped in inward and outward spiritual assistance from You and him.

Being with Allah and His Messenger ﷺ

Ḥabīb ʻUmar bin Hafīẓ (may Allah protect him and benefit us through him) reflects upon the meaning of being with Allah and His Messenger ﷺ. Extracts from a lesson in Ihya ʻUlum al-Din in Dar al-Mustafa, Tarim, on 9th Rabiʼ al-Awwal 1436 /31st December 2014

The Messenger of Allah ﷺ said: "A person is with the one they love." Thus, you can gauge your love for Allah and His Messenger by gauging how much you are with them.

The Prophet was in the highest state of being with his Lord. For that reason, he said: "I am nothing but a slave. I eat as a slave eats and I sit as a slave sits."

Sayyiduna Ibrahim says in the Qur'an that it is his Lord: "Who created me, and it is He who guides me; Who gives me food and drink." He was constantly with Allah, even when he ate and drank.

One of the Knowers of Allah said: "For twenty years people think I have been speaking to them, when in reality I have been speaking to Allah." If you speak for His sake, in accordance with His Sacred Law and your heart is present with Him, then in reality you are speaking to Him.

The Companions and the pious people of this Ummah were constantly with the Messenger of Allah ﷺ in all their states. One of the Companions repeated three times, addressing the Prophet ﷺ: "I love Allah and His Messenger!" He replied ﷺ on each occasion: "You are with the one you love."

Sayyiduna Abu'l-'Abbas al-Mursi said: "If the Prophet ﷺ was absent from me for an instant I would not consider myself a Muslim."

Ḥabīb 'Umar bin 'Abd al-Rahman al-'Attas asked: "How can he be absent from us when he is the source of our existence?"

In other words, without him, we do not exist.

Imam al-Haddad said:

وَلِي من رسولِ اللهِ جَدِّي عِنَايَةٌ

وَوَجْهٌ وَإِمْدَادٌ وَإِرْثٌ وَإِيثَارُ

'I receive from my grandfather, the Messenger of Allah, care, status, assistance, inheritance and preferential treatment.'

These people reached the highest stations of being with the Beloved ﷺ.

So do not claim to love him and then depart from him. Are you with him in emulating his character? If you truly loved him, you would be with him. Do you think being with him is only in the next life? That which will be manifest in the next life is only that which is stored up in this life. If you want to be with him there, be certain that you have to be with him here.

How long have you been with your lower self (nafs)? It calls you to base things while Allah and His Messenger ﷺ call you to lofty things. Your lower self calls you to the Fire, while they call you to Paradise. Being with Allah and His Messenger ﷺ is better than being with your lower self. Your lower self is the thing which cuts you off most from being with Allah and His Messenger and it is the biggest veil between you and your Lord.

Printed in Great Britain
by Amazon

71510047R00052